ANIMAL ALPHABET

priddy books

A is for alligator

B is for bear

c is for cat

D is for dinosaurs

E is for elephants

F is for fox

G is for goat

H is for horse

I is for insects

J is for
jellyfish

K is for
kitten

L is for lion

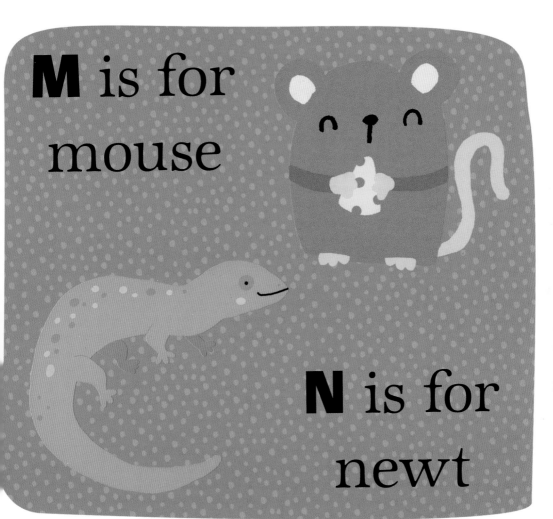

M is for mouse

N is for newt

o is for octopus

P is for penguin

Q is for queen bee

R is for
rooster

S is for
snake

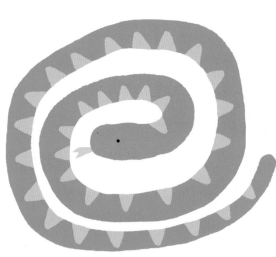

T is for tortoise

u is for unicorn

V is for
vulture

W is for
whale

X is for

x-ray fish

Y is for

yak

z is for zebra

Aa Bb Cc Dd Ee
Ff Gg Hh Ii Jj Kk
Ll Mm Nn Oo Pp
Qq Rr Ss Tt Uu
Vv Ww Xx Yy Zz